But She Is Also Jane

BUT SHE IS ALSO JANE

LAURA READ

UNIVERSITY OF MASSACHUSETTS PRESS
Amherst and Boston

Copyright © 2023 by University of Massachusetts Press
All rights reserved
Printed in the United States of America

ISBN 978-1-62534-714-5 (paper)

Designed by Deste Roosa
Set in Adobe Jenson Pro and Fiorello
Printed and bound by Books International, Inc.

Cover design by adam b. bohannon
Cover image by Jane Maxwell, *Girl Interrupted*, mixed media with resin on panel,
© 2012. Courtesy of the artist.

Library of Congress Cataloging-in-Publication Data
Names: Read, Laura, author.
Title: But she is also Jane / Laura Read.
Description: Amherst ; Boston : University of Massachusetts Press, [2023] |
    Series: Juniper prize for poetry
Identifiers: LCCN 2022044968 (print) | LCCN 2022044969 (ebook) | ISBN
    9781625347145 (paperback) | ISBN 9781685750138 (ebook)
Subjects: LCGFT: Poetry.
Classification: LCC PS3618.E224 B88 2023 (print) | LCC PS3618.E224
    (ebook) | DDC 811/.6—dc23/eng/20220923
LC record available at https://lccn.loc.gov/2022044968
LC ebook record available at https://lccn.loc.gov/2022044969

British Library Cataloguing-in-Publication Data
A catalog record for this book is available from the British Library.

*for Maya Miller and Margaret Corinne,
and also Jane*

My heroine would be myself, only in disguise.
—*Esther Greenwood, from Sylvia Plath's* The Bell Jar

CONTENTS

I

II

But She Is Also Jane

I

RIP, Laura's Vagina

Your vagina is beginning to devitalize,
the doctor explained, when I asked him why
I had had so many urinary tract infections lately.
The first thing I thought was that I should say
No, your vagina is devitalizing, because I have
two teenage sons, and that is what passes for wit
in our house. But then I got lost in the fact
that he didn't, in fact, have a vagina.
Then, in the little room inside my mind
where Dorothy Parker was holding court
at the Algonquin, I thought maybe *devitalize*
is just a medical term, give the guy a break.
But I didn't even know this man.
Couldn't he just give me a prescription
and say something vague about aging?
What about euphemism? I guess *devitalize*
was one because he went on to more vividly
explain that my tissues were, frankly, deteriorating.
At that point, I was thinking *But you haven't even*
seen the area in question and *How did you get*
this far without knowing how to talk to women?
Devitalize reminds me of de-ice which is what
I was doing just before this tricky moment
at the Urgent Care. My son was late to algebra
because it's really cold and it took a while
to clean the car. And at 8:00 the door
where he usually goes in automatically locks,
so I had to take him around to the front,
and he dropped his phone in the snow
and it got run over, so now there's a crack
in the screen. He wants me to replace it,
but I said, *No, it still works.*

Music Box

I am good at getting knots out of necklaces.
I have small fingers.
Which means I am bad at reaching an octave.
Is everything good also bad?
People think I'm not strong, but I am.
I can cook Italian like my grandmother Marie
who loved roses. Like Marie
in her nursing home in Brooklyn.
My brother drove us.
I am not good at driving. But I am good
at knowing a face even when
it's vacant and sunk into a melting body.
I am good at bending down and whispering
who I am. At finding a picture
tucked away in a drawer and wondering
if it was a nurse or Marie
who put it there.
I wouldn't want to look at it either.
It is of all of us at the pool in our swimsuits,
the sun licking our legs and making patterns
on the water.
I am good at remembering.
I am a silver box shaped like a piano
and lined with velvet.
You can keep your earrings inside me,
or a folded note.
I'm a grand piano. I take up a whole room.
On the part that opens, there's a mirror.
I am not a music box, even though
I am a box shaped like music.
The music you have to imagine.

The Milkmaid

I bought a stoneware bowl with three pansies
on it without thinking it was because
we had plates with pansies in those first years,
but it was.

Do you remember where you saw it last?
is an infuriating question and fills
my mind with bells.

I also didn't remember that we had a print
of *The Milkmaid* by Vermeer until
I saw it hanging over our couch in an old photo.

For years I thought I had been drawn to it
because I like the domestic interior.

The girl in the painting is making bread pudding.
She is pouring milk into a bowl.

She is concentrating because you have to use
just the right amount of milk,
so I am concentrating too.

This is both intense and relaxing.
Like sex, which the painting is also about.

The floor tiles have cupids on them,
and there's a foot warmer in the corner,
which the girl might put under her skirt,
and she is smiling to herself.

I didn't know that at the bottom of everything
is sex and my first house.

I thought I just bought the bowl with the pansies
because I wanted it

and that I always stop when I see *The Milkmaid*
because I like to watch her pour the milk,
carefully and slow.

Jellyfish

In Victoria, we watched from the rocks
as the jellyfish floated towards us.

A jellyfish has no brain so its thoughts
are different, tentacles trailing from its head

like ribbons, like something shredded,
like what you say but shouldn't.

I thought if I touched one, I would never
stop. I thought I wanted to be stung.

My mother wore a long blue dress.
She had brought a man with us.

My eyelids were heavy from watching.
We slept in a trailer with the sea

on one side and the hills on the other
and inside the hills were goats

with bells on their necks.
Jellyfish bloom suddenly and in large

numbers. Like when you turn a doorknob
and the room comes rushing towards you,

all its lamps and clocks.
This woman was not my mother.

She hummed to herself.
She glowed underwater.

She used her body to propel herself forward.
The moon jelly swarms, which implies

an active ability to stay together.
The moon jelly is also called *Aurelia*.

Everything has another name.
In Victoria, I did not yet know

my own secrets. That I think with my body
and this means I am not good.

That it's dark and the hills are ringing
and I am silent and twisting inside the sea.

That what stings is beautiful.
That what is beautiful stings.

Jane Doe 1–9

The president of my college has been accused by nine Jane Does.

Jane Doe is what we call an unidentified body.

One Jane says he put his hand on her breast.

One Jane says he showed her his penis.

One Jane took notes of everything he said and did.

Smart girl, he might have said.

The road I drive to the college is lined with evergreens.

It's not that evergreens don't lose their needles

but that they replace them quickly.

My mother's name is Jane. She was an only child.

Lonely in the woods of childhood.

I read mysteries inside that silence, stared at a shaft of light

where you could see particles of dust.

I couldn't believe I hadn't known they were there.

One Jane says, *Of course she did not come forward.*

Would we have believed her?

One Jane said, *Don't walk home in the darkness.*

One Jane said, *Yes, she had sex with him but she was afraid for her job.*

One Jane said he texted her 559 times in one day.

One Jane destroyed the records.

One Jane taught me how to read, sketch of a girl on an empty page

with her brother Dick and their dog Spot.

I liked how only some of the page was picture.

People can appear from out of nowhere.

There's also a younger girl in a red wagon.

Jane is pulling her.

But she is also Jane.

Erin

Erin is sitting on the floor
of our dorm room.
Erin with the thick red braid
and the freckles the sun had tossed
across her face. Erin who is pretty
and brave and knows how to talk to boys
and knows that the party we are going to
fills my mouth with a metal taste
like you get from a school drinking fountain
so she brings me a plastic cup from the keg.

The room for aerobics is lined with mirrors.
I stand in the back row
so I can follow the other girls,
so I will only see their bodies in the room
and the mirror, not my own.
In the front row, in the corner,
there's a girl who looks like a stick drawing,
the kind I do with the kids I babysit
because I don't know how to make a real body.
I am thinking this when the girl turns.

Erin still likes school.
In class, we write down everything
the professor says. When he tells us
that in literature *to die* means
to have an orgasm,
we are embarrassed but we also think
he is beautiful. We sit in the grass
with our textbooks open. She teaches me
how to open the stem of a dandelion
and push another one through.

Erin visits me in France
and because other women do it,
and men even, we walk through
the whole city with our arms linked.
I can't think of anything
but how her arm is touching mine.

I visit her in the hospital.
I bring balloons.
Her hair is feathers, her body driftwood.
There are no mirrors.

I get drunk at Erin's wedding
and cry on her white dress
which has beads that hurt my eyes
and I think I leave a smear of mascara.
This is what it will always be.
She never speaks to me again.

Solving for X

Whether I should say *You taught me algebra*
to the woman I recognize in the YMCA bathroom

is a dilemma. That is to say, it is a problem
that is not easy to solve.

I like the way *solve* means to break
something down, as in *dissolve*, or *solvent*.

I want to tell Mrs. Hicks that I always liked
her tightly coiled hair that could not be

controlled and that that's how I recognized her,
and also that I appreciated how calm she was

when explaining a problem that would cause me
to panic from knowing so little or now

from having forgotten so much.
When I was in her class, I was fourteen

and had mononucleosis.
My teachers agreed that algebra was the only

homework I had to do before I went to bed.
My mother had a new baby, and he cried like scissors

cutting through my sleep, making a shape of it.
I used to sew. I used to pin tissue paper patterns

to fabric. I used to solve for x.
Once a girl was wearing a white skirt

and got her period and Mrs. Hicks made us
all put our heads down like we were playing

Heads Up 7 Up in elementary school
so the girl could walk out.

I don't want to undress in front of Mrs. Hicks,
though I know she doesn't know me.

She looks tired and is staring into
her empty locker like a mind.

I put on my coat and smile as if I am
just a random middle-aged woman

and she a random older one
and there has never been anything between us,

no invisible numbers we were trying to pin down.
I don't ask if she remembers the boy I stared at

all during her class who was always getting up
to sharpen his pencil as if he just couldn't work

in these conditions. Or if she ever thought about
how *Heads Up 7 Up* is a game that is weirdly based

on figuring out who touched you
when you were not allowed to look.

The Whole History of Femininity

At your wedding, you lifted up your dress
so I could attach your garter belt to your stockings.

My hand was shaking even though we still had
the strange intimacy of girls.

You had to reach around and clip the belt yourself.
I failed you and the whole history of femininity.

But we lived in a time of elastic.
The only problem with pantyhose was how easily

they tore, but you could paint over a hole
with clear fingernail polish.

It was still a hole, but it didn't get any larger.
Did you know at weddings people used to tackle

the bride to remove the garter?
Do men like all those belts and clips

so they feel like they're finding something hidden,
something that is theirs alone?

I drove ten hours to your wedding in a borrowed car.
When you visited me the next year,

I was eating only grapes and English muffin pizzas.
My heart was beating fast like when you jump

in a cold lake and at first you think you might die.
I went to the doctor and he said I had something called

costochondritis and hooked me up to a machine
that sent electric currents across my chest.

I know now I was just hungry.
Since then, I have never let anyone touch

that spot between my breasts.

"In the same way we misunderstand the child ballerinas of Degas"

In every alley of the theatre loom the silhouettes of portly gentlemen
in top hats who have come to take their pleasure with these skinny
half-naked adolescents. They too will have learned to mime desire.

—*Germaine Greer*

But what if they have come instead to make pleasure
by force? Sometimes the body flushes
when it shouldn't. Someone says,
I am going to teach you something.
In college, I kept buying posters of women lying down.
I didn't notice until I was lying down
and saw them all at once.
Some of them were dead. Like Ophelia.
Or the woman in the moat with the man on the horse
in the background. It wasn't clear if he had put
her there or had come to get her out.
Edgar Degas did not paint girls lying down.
He liked women at work: milliners, laundresses,
dancers backstage, bending and stretching.
Women alone, women who didn't want to be watched.
Or did they? I want you to notice me tucking this curl
behind my ear, widening my eyes in a way
you might find becoming, exhaling so my chest rises
and falls a little and you think of a breeze lifting
a curtain. But you should also know that I'm serious.
I like how Degas washed a whole room of dancers
in green or blue. How the tint of the shadow depended
on what they were doing with their bodies
on that particular day in that particular room,

how beauty is the same in its costume but also
slightly different each moment,
like how that leaf fell on your hair and startled you.
Degas was anti-Semitic.
In a discussion of beauty, let us not forget ugliness.
The boy bagged groceries. He put everything
on my mother's list into the bag with his hands
while his eyes pinned mine to his
and his lips smiled like he was pleased
with the way the sun looked going down
over the field he'd just harvested.

The Lucky Penny

Once I was drinking at the Lucky Penny
with a woman named Becky.
We waited tables together.
She was small but could carry those big trays
that hold six plates.
Becky took me to bars where I never went
on my own. But this bar
was where I used to drink in college.
So I sat down next to my girl self
on a wobbly stool.
She looked like she was just playing
at sorrow. When she asked if she could
go to his apartment to see
what he was doing, I said, *Why not?*
She said she would run the whole way
and look in and then run right back.
What I like about an Edward Hopper painting
is that it's an open window.
He was making a sandwich,
sweeping a knife across a piece of bread,
and he didn't look up.
The lamp he would break was still whole.
For once, he was innocent.
When she came back, she said all the lights
in the apartment were on
and I said it's just like Hopper,
but she didn't understand.
I said it was just a room with a person in it
whose feelings rose in his face for a moment.

Is it to preserve the heat of the body?

Sometimes that flamingo your grandmother
stuck in the mud of your midwestern yard

comes to me like an old friend
and I am full of what is not quite

longing as it would not hold up
under examination of what I really want

but something that resembles it enough.
The woman next to me on the plane and I

have a silent agreement: she can twirl her hair
endlessly while I bite my fourth fingernail.

We both look straight ahead and do not talk
even when Dion comes to ask us what

we'd like to drink, Dion who wants us
to call him Dion, so I feel like somehow

we are close. I get the red wine for the drama,
the red filled to the lip of the plastic cup,

the kind of cup you are sometimes asked
to pee in. By sometimes, I mean like when

a child might be inside you, which is important
to find out. No one is inside me now.

Once I went to visit you in Omaha
where the flamingo stood on its one leg,

famously. We don't know why they do it—
is it to preserve the heat of the body?

One scientist has devoted his entire life
to studying this. I think that is a great use

of a life, and I am wondering
what I have done with my own.

I know I haven't seen you in a while.
You're a pilot, so you could be flying this plane

I'm on. I think it would be difficult to sleep
standing on one leg, but then

I am not a flamingo. I also would not like
being pink, or plastic, or sitting in a yard,

trying to be cheerful and remind everyone
that there are other places with other birds,

fantastic pink ones who do things we may never
understand. And also, we may never see

the real ones. If I do see you again, I might ask
if you've looked in the mirror and thought

your face has grown so different but also
has stayed kind of the same

and wondered which thought is right?
We will probably never see each other again

and have that moment when you say nothing
but think of the whole life you didn't live

that sits inside the one you did.
This is probably what the flamingos

are doing. I know that is where I go
when I close my eyes and pull my body close.

The Pea

I liked it when my mother had her hysterectomy
and we sat on her king-sized bed,
folding clothes and watching *Mork and Mindy.*

If any of my brothers came in,
we pointed at the door.

Every night after dinner, I cleaned the floor
on my hands and knees even though
she couldn't come downstairs to check.

I thought somehow she would know if I didn't,
like the princess and the pea.

My boyfriend had a black truck.
He washed it so often it shone.

We had just graduated from college
and were working at a day camp together
when he broke up with me.

I quit that night because I couldn't
get back in that truck even one more time

even though I had girls waiting
to eat their sack lunches next to me,
their sticky fingers touching my arms.

I loved the end of each episode
when Mork checks in with Orson.

I liked the way he told him all the weird
things we were doing here on Earth.
It's difficult to think of this show now

without thinking of Robin Williams's body
in that white bag.

People wondered how someone that funny
could be so sad, but isn't that like saying,
How did your child get so tall?

In my boyfriend's truck, I sometimes sat
with one leg on either side of the stick shift

to remind him why he liked me.
Having a boyfriend was what
I'd always wanted.

My mother was interested in women
having their own power.

It was weird to sit on that bed and know
something was gone inside her,

something we didn't think about much
when it was there.

But it was a new world now.

The Cheerleader

I can't decide if it is something to be ashamed of
or proud. It could mean I gave up integrity
for affirmation. That I was pretty and popular
enough. It could undermine my desire for people
in the present to consider me smart. Which is insulting
to me and other cheerleaders and also to my audience.
I had an appliqué with my name on it
and one with a bullpup because that was our mascot,
I had a letter sweater like it was the 1950s
because I considered letter jackets
too bulky and masculine. I had designed myself to be
feminine. This was before I understood that gender
was a construct and a performance, when I thought
it was a ticket to love. I have been asked why
I was a cheerleader with a curiosity pretending
to contain no judgment and I said because I was young,
because I liked to dance, because I wanted to fit in,
because it was fun to stand on the wall at Albi Stadium
and whisper and laugh with the other girls
who had been set apart by our blue and white uniforms.
I said, *Don't pretend you don't think it's beneath
or above you.* You would have liked Fridays too,
when we wore our uniforms to school to advertise
for the game, so we didn't have to sort through
all the other choices of what kind of image we wanted
to project like a film, or the slide shows my dad
used to make on the dining room wall.
Look at me and Tom when we camped in Banff
and he tricked us when we hiked all the way up
to the teahouse and said he forgot his wallet but really
he had a twenty tucked into his magic belt.
Look at Chris. No one wonders, I guess,
why we're looking at so many pictures of him

when he was only two and very sick and on medication
that made his face break out and his eyes and lips
always wet from crying. He wore a cute blue sleeper
that had once belonged to his brothers
so he didn't look so different.
He rode his Toddler Taxi through the kitchen.
Sometimes you can see me in the corner of a picture,
coming in and out because I was so much older and already
a cheerleader. Sometimes it's even Friday and I'm in
my uniform with my name and my bullpup
and the promise of the evening hovering in front of me
like the horizon. I didn't understand the horizon.
Sometimes I would run and run far from the house,
trying to get closer to its vibrating light,
but this proved impossible, which I guess is science.
Maybe you think what a cheerleader move
to not understand the horizon. Or maybe I'm projecting.
It's important to put everything up on the wall.

Maya Miller

You should have seen how Maya looked
running across the field.

We had glimpsed a moose on the other side
of the waterfall and she said we could find him
if we took off our shoes and walked through the creek.
She ran ahead. She looked like she was bounding.
She yelled back, *This is what it was like*
being my friend when I was 14.

Last week, my husband visited the graves.
He could not find my father
even with the map, even when the man
from the cemetery office came and stuck
his spade down until he hit my father's stone,
which had been buried over.
Even though I wasn't there, I keep thinking
about the sound of the shovel hitting the stone.

We did not find the moose.
When we got up to the ridge and looked down,
we realized the way we should have gone.

When Maya was 14, her name was Maya Miller.
When I was 14, I sat on my brown-flowered couch
and dreamed of being a girl like Maya,
who always had scratches on her legs
from where the fields had touched her.

This week I read a poem that said poetry
is about telling the truth.
This week I noticed all the rhododendrons
rising up against their houses.
It is late May and this is their moment.

Supposedly we all have one,
and this may be mine.

I saw the moose across the field,
and at least I tried to find him.

Margaret Corinne, Dunseith, North Dakota, 1932

We sit and wait, my sister-in-law says at the deathbed
and I do all day, I am dutiful, I remember the hot church
and the fat angels on the altar and the fan oscillating

by the woman who led us in singing, with one hand
always up in the air. No one knows I am thinking,
Die, die as everyone talks about Jesus and the better place

she is going. Last week my husband pointed at something
invisible and said, *Here is the mind,* and then he pointed
in the opposite direction and said, *And here is you,*

and I said, *With the daisies,* pointing to the same spot
in the air and loving myself hard for seeing a whole field
of them there. But I love myself less when evening comes

and his mother is still drawing her endless breaths up
through her ribs and I can't sit anymore, I am thinking
about the window and how I have to get outside.

I am neither Mary nor Martha. No small pitcher
of water to wash her feet, no sponge for her lips.
When we were alone, I told her things she already knew,

like we were in a play and the audience needed filling in
on what had already happened. She was a good mother.
In her bathroom cupboard, she had the oldest jar

of Vaseline I'd ever seen. A bottle of Emeraude,
green like Oz or something you could drink, the kind
of perfume you tilt and touch to your wrist.

I said, *Don't worry, they've still drawn your eyebrows on,*
and now I must tell you that all her life she shaved them
and penciled in thick, black lines, she put on a face

because when she was the girl in the photograph,
standing in the cold sunlight of Dunseith, North Dakota,
at the age of three, a stern brother on either side,

she learned she was nothing. And now she is whittled
down to bones and I can see the small flame
of her childhood not going out. I lift the covers

and she is wearing almost nothing and her skin
is so thin that even the sheet bruises it so we shape it
like a tent. As a girl I liked to pretend my sheets

were a meadow where the Velveteen Rabbit lived
and all the other animals I was making real
with my love and my fever, but I didn't think of how

they would have to be burned. This is what happens
with love, I tell her, as I picture the fire swallowing
her body piece by piece, the way sometimes people

eat paper to destroy evidence. I didn't know in death
the jaw sticks open, that the world would keep falling
into it, that we would continue talking to her as if

she could hear us, that my husband would ask
all of us to leave him alone with her for a minute
before they took her body so he could tell her

something secret, like when Joan of Arc
whispered something in the ear of the dauphin,
something we'll never know.

Yesterday

Yesterday I wondered why everyone is always writing
about how wild they were or were not in the brief years
before they weren't. By everyone I mean me.
All my poems are about the boys I wanted to kiss
and the ash I flicked off that one cigarette.
One may be an understatement. Shouldn't I try to be
more exact? Yesterday at 10:00 a.m., Henry would not
quit barking at the front window and I thought,
Stop bragging about what you think you're capable of.
Just lie down. It might not have been 10:00 a.m..
And Henry might have barked even if I wasn't home.
The way I'm writing this poem because I'm awake
and shut in this body and a little angry and I want you
to know. Or I wanted you to. Yesterday. I see why
the Beatles believed in it. It's over so now it's real.
Like my mother-in-law who just died so her things
are strewn all over our living room. Her box of scarves,
her painting of Jesus, her clock with the broken hands.
No wonder Henry is barking. Isn't she suddenly
here again in the chair, smoking and drinking
the way we all did when we were young?
She hasn't been this alive in years.

Deer are the obvious stand-ins for the dead

which is why I followed
two of them through the Samish Island
Community of Christ campground

where I was because it's where
my husband used to go
with his brother and his mother,

both of whom are now dead.
I forgot to explain, though it is
probably unnecessary, why deer

are the perfect manifestation:
it's their knobby knees and slender
legs, their fragility and strength,

the way they stop only for a moment
to look in your eyes in that way
it takes a whole lifetime to find

and the way you know they are about
to go. I found them at the top
of the trail I was following down

to the beach where I remember
Brad's brother and his wife and child
running when we had the car all

packed and ready to go and I was hungry
and wanted to go out for lunch
but they wanted to have a Moment,

which I found a little overly
constructed but is exactly what
I'm doing now. I picked a wild rose

and left it on a bench.
It was starting to rain, which fits in
nicely. What doesn't fit is the two deer

I saw individually on my way home,
each one's head twisted back
by the car that had hit it and left it

lying there on the road
as if to say there was no wild rose
or beach or rain. Some nights I dream

that someone wakes me
and says, *Why aren't you packed?*
We're leaving for Paris!

The person is dumping my clothes
into a giant suitcase and looking
for my passport. I only have the one

from when I went last, when I was 20,
so we decide I'll just wear sunglasses,
which is fine because I like to keep

the years to myself.
Often what I want is impossible
like going back to Paris again and also

never returning to that city where
my throat filled with dust from speaking
to no one. This time all the clothes

I packed are red so here I am in Paris,
frightened and obvious.
If you see me like this, you will know

we are in my dream together
and that you should follow me
because I am a sign.

Neither Bride nor Daughter

Once I went to a kegger at my childhood home.
I didn't know I was going but Jen was sitting
on her dresser listening to the Eagles
and curling her hair and then we were walking
through the dark neighborhood and then
we were on my porch and someone
was handing me a plastic cup.
I said, *This is my porch*, and he laughed
and said, *Mine too*, but it wasn't.
He didn't know there was supposed to be
a brown-flowered couch in the living room
and over the mantel, a print of a Rembrandt
called *The Jewish Bride*, 1655.
For all of childhood, it hung there
and I never knew what it was called or why,
how an art dealer said it was a father giving
a necklace to his daughter for her wedding,
but how most art historians now think
it is actually Isaac and Rebecca.
There was another keg in my room
in the basement. Strangers were moving
between my invisible bed and my stereo,
stepping over my clothes on the floor,
staring at themselves in my mirror,
wondering if they will ever be good enough.
The water rushed through the pipes
and the furnace made that sound
like it used to. I had to stand in the corner,
drinking and singing both parts
of "Total Eclipse of the Heart,"
holding the note at the end of *Turn around*,

bright eyes long enough to imply it was still
going when I started *Every now and then*
I fall apart. This was the song I listened to
late at night while I waited for you
to come pick me up so we could drive through
the empty streets in the dark.
Years later, you sent me a picture
of that house to show me you remembered
where it was. In the painting,
the man and the woman
are not looking at each other.
I like it when one thing covers another
but not completely, like fog.
Rembrandt was famous for his ability
to concentrate light. In the painting,
the light shines on the man's palm
touching the woman's chest.
Everything else is dark.

II

Quince

I dreamed a man cut my hair before I could say
yes or no. I didn't know whether to say yes
or no. I still don't. He cut it in the kind of steps

that look like terraces. That doesn't work for curls
but it feels good when the scissors are actually
doing the thing you've feared and wanted.

I used to wear my hair short because that's what
my mother thought I should do. She said
I was an autumn and didn't look good in red,

and that I should marry someone rich because
I couldn't take care of myself. She wasn't wrong,
and she meant to be kind. Once she pointed at a picture

of a panda sleeping and said it reminded her of me
because I'd always known how to relax.
It was something she wouldn't do but she'd come

to understand it could have some virtue.
My hair makes me look like the girl who lived
in the apartment with the boy who stole her money

for drugs. She both knew and she didn't.
She liked his arm around her in the dark, making
the night feel harmless. Seeing myself like this again

makes me almost forgive her. When she finally
kicked him out, she listened to that song
by The Replacements about the black-eyed Susans.

She'd never even seen a black-eyed Susan or at least
she'd never seen one and known that's what it was.
Yesterday I drove to a farm with a woman

who was looking for quince. She knew how much
you should put in a pie to make the apples taste
a little richer. When a man asked us what kind of apples

we wanted, she said, *Empire,* as if that was the only answer.
If a man cut her hair in a dream, she would wake up
and think, *Yes, that is exactly right.*

Clever Dress

I bought a new dress. It's called a shift,
which means it's all one piece.

It's deceiving because the top half is black and the bottom
is black and white plaid.

Not plaid exactly. A pattern like the static
on an old television, which people used to call snow.

Televisions had this kind of static
when you got stuck between channels.

Whenever I buy something new,
I hang it in the front of my closet,

which I can see from my bed.
I like to stare at it in the dark and consider it.

I did this last night, and I thought of the snow, and suddenly
everything was obvious.

When I tried it on at the store, I felt exactly
like myself. The skirt was short, and I was wearing

black leggings and short black boots
like the kind I had in high school.

Some things belong to you, and if you're lucky,
you get them back.

Last night my friend called to say she hoped I wasn't mad
so I said I wasn't but I was.

I didn't even know until this morning
when I woke up with a little paperweight on my chest,

the kind I used to have for my desk.
You didn't want your papers to get scattered.

I am so talented at telling myself what is true
and then believing it that I can shock myself.

Have you ever watched a person you love
get caught in a lie, a big lie like they are not really

who they said? You know the way they rearrange
their face so it will look like the face you knew before

but you know now it never was?
Imagine that face is your own.

Imagine you think you are not mad
and then you wake up.

I also had a desk set, which looked like an open book
with a leather border around a calendar.

You could put your cup of pens to the right
and your paperweight to the left.

At first, I thought the dress was two pieces.
Clever dress.

Elegy with Sammy Hagar and *Beauty and the Beast*

Aren't you astonished when the tiny lifeboat of your mind
surfaces in annoyance at how much the vice president
of the college where you're about to leave your son

is belaboring his point? At how, when you're sobbing
so hard in the car as you're driving off,
you can also imagine how maybe later you could buy

some of those yogurt-covered pretzels at the gas station
because isn't this one of those days you've been
waiting for all your life when it's okay to have

what you want? You know how the only good thing
about someone being in the hospital is sitting
in a diner late at night and eating pancakes with syrup,

slowly lifting the fork to your mouth?
The body carries on its little dramas.
There is life without you.

It's like after someone dies and every moment
is a moment you live and he didn't.
At this point, you might be thinking you should

remind me that my son is not dead, but I wouldn't.
Not after the gas station did not have the pretzels.
Not after trying to listen to music and getting

what I used to call, and I guess still do,
that Sammy Hagar feeling, which means Sammy
is playing his guitar too loud in his room and you want

to tell him to turn it down or just move out already,
a feeling I never had with you.
I can't believe you will have so many thoughts now

that I don't know about. It's like the first time
I realized your mind had its privacy.
You were sitting at the table on your booster seat, coloring,

and you looked up and said, *Mom, do you think I'm odd?*
And then a few minutes later,
Mom, are you happy here with me?

Later, I realized both these lines were from
Beauty and the Beast, that you were acting, and that you
realized this and didn't tell me, that you knew

they belonged to the movie but now also to you,
and I asked you about it and a smile slid across your lips
the way smoke moves, and I could see your intelligence

and the little corridors behind your eyes
you would walk down until you reached the door
you've opened now. And me too, I want to tell you,

I am having thoughts of my own, I am thinking of when
I moved into my dorm and Bobby McFerrin was singing,
"Don't worry, be happy" on the radio,

and my roommate had tied a piece of fabric softener
to the fan, which was something I'd never seen before
and made the air smell so good.

We're out of tin, we have aluminum

Once I asked Matthew to get me some tinfoil
from the drawer and he peeked his head around

the doorframe and sang me a little song,
We're out of tin, we have aluminum.

I wish I could sing it for you
but you are probably reading this alone

in your living room or not reading it at all
and anyway, I can't get that little boy voice

exactly right. Did you know that aluminum
was discovered in Denmark in 1825?

I wish I knew that story.
Who was walking through beautiful Scandinavia

and saw a little shine stuck in a fist of rock
and thought we could use that to bake potatoes?

What I know about baking potatoes
is that you have to make sure the shiny side

is out. Yesterday I went to the planetarium
where I learned I get dizzy when I look

too long at the stars, at least the fake stars
which are moving faster than the real stars do,

those fixed little doorknobs.
I also learned that all elements are made

from the death of stars. When a star dies,
it scatters its body through space and those elements

then float around for a while, say a million years,
and then they are collected into a new star

and pieces break off into planets,
like the one we're on right now.

It's important not to forget
when you're thinking about how

you can't sleep because your children
are no longer upstairs

that you are on a planet with hidden elements
everywhere from stars that died a long time

before you were even born.
The difference between tin and aluminum

is that tin is very rare.
No wonder Matthew couldn't find it.

Aluminum is the 3rd most common
element and tin the 49th.

It's like that sometimes, isn't it?
The house is so quiet now.

The Fourth Wall

Some days we're obviously
in a show, like when my son comes home
from college and I forget he is special
and finish what I was doing before saying hello.
The first hours he's home,
I have to remind myself
every time I come out of my bedroom
that I'm playing the role of his mother.
I go to my bedroom a lot,
like a woman from the 1950s who has to lie down.
My son wears a heart monitor now
so the doctors can follow
his ventricular tachycardia, which is a term
I just learned that means that your heart races
and you get lightheaded and sometimes
results in sudden death.
I think it's incredible that people I've never met
are watching my son's heart
from 300 miles away
when sometimes I can't even remember
to be his mother.
I heard his heart beat when he was inside of me
and it was, of course, miraculous
and loud, like the ocean inside a shell,
which people tell me they can hear.
Actually, it was more like a horse galloping
towards you, another thing I've never heard
though at camp we slapped our hands quickly
on our knees to make a sound just like it,
and it was exciting,
summoning those invisible horses.
Lately, on the shows I'm not in but like to watch,
everyone's been breaking the fourth wall,

which I enjoy—a character looks at you
through the screen and invites you,
with just the lift of an eyebrow,
to see the world as she does.
It's easier to be in the show if you're able
to step out of it
like this.

Phallogocentric

At the spring quarter composition meeting,
my male colleague runs up to the board
and writes the word, *phallogocentric,*
and then explains that the essay
in the Western tradition is phallic.
He says we should tell our students this
so they know the tradition they're writing in.
I raise my hand and wait for a long time
to be called on and when I am,
the Director of Composition apologizes,
and I say, *It's no problem, I've just been
waiting patiently like a woman,*
which I thought would draw a laugh,
but, apparently, there are some things
about which we should be honest,
and others we shouldn't.
I say I am not going to tell my students that
and then ask them to follow the rules
we just questioned. Why not say
the main idea can be arrived at?
Or maybe there is no main idea?
Maybe there are so many little ideas
sticking out like curls that won't be
brushed down. I know you can't brush curls—
doesn't everyone who has them?
You have to use leave-in conditioner
and product and scrunch them
and then try not to touch them
or they will break and turn to frizz
and then where will you be?
All week now, I've been thinking of this word,
phallogocentric, which my friend said
Derrida invented and Wikipedia says

is a portmanteau, which I guess
is a blending of two words
but which I thought was a suitcase.
I love suitcases. I love the satiny lining
and the clasps and how they make me think
of trains and steam and hoopskirts
and top hats. How did I get here?
Does it matter? Will I arrive?
I don't know but out the window
voila! the whole French countryside
that Derrida once flew past while he thought
about masculinity and language.
Sometimes I think about dying
and what I see is the white sheet
my boyfriend and I washed
and draped over our balcony in Nice.
We left it there to dry and walked
through the city and ate chocolate,
and climbed up the hill and looked out over
the Mediterranean, which is so many shades
of blue and green you can't imagine,
and he smoked a pipe, which I think
made him feel more like a man,
something I couldn't say then
but I could now if I could find him.
Would he laugh? Would he remember
how when we got back, the sheet was dry
and perfectly white and looked like
nothing had happened?

American Realism

Here is what happened:
I was staring at the man on the train whose eyes
had been emptied out like pockets and then not
tucked back in.
I couldn't look away. His hair was long
and receding high up on his forehead.
He was so thin that when he stood up,
his pants came all the way down.
He didn't notice.
The man sitting next to me, clothed and sober,
looked at me because it was only the two men
and me on the train.
He started to get up to tell the other man
about his pants but then
the man pulled them up himself.

Here is how I told the story to a man:
it was weird. It was no big deal.
I felt bad for the man. And then after,
I went to the American Realism exhibit
at the art museum where I saw a painting
called *Hibernation*. It was a picture of a mink
sleeping inside a series of intersecting circles.
At first, I didn't even see the mink,
just the circles, which were very large
and pink and looked like energy.
I also saw a painting called *Annunciation*
in which two women are talking in a bathroom
that looks just like the bathroom
in my high school. One is wearing a blue slip
and the other is barefoot and leaning up
against a wall, thinking about something
the blue slip woman has just told her.

Later I told the story of the man
losing his pants on the train to a woman.
That time I told it this way: I was frightened.
Because exposing the body can be an act
of violence. Because he was barely aware
that his body was something he still lived inside.
I know the man meant no harm,
he meant nothing at all, I should just be sad
for him, which I was and am.
But I live inside a series of circles,
so many you might not see me at first,
or think it's my story at all.

Marie Curie and the Isotopes, World Tour, 1911

is what my new t-shirt that I got for Christmas says
under her picture.

When I unwrapped it, my son was mysteriously
exasperated and asked why I like Marie Curie so much

anyway, which oddly I was unprepared to answer.
I think I said that winter in Paris when she wore

everything she owned to stay warm in her attic room
while she nobly studied chemistry

for the good of all of us, or maybe Pierre's head
crushed by the wheel of a carriage

leaving her to raise Irene and Eve on her own
or how she left them home alone at night

while she went to the laboratory to finish the work
she and Pierre had started or how she and Irene

dragged their X-ray machine onto the fields of WWI
to help the soldiers or maybe her hands rotting

and killing her or the glowing journal
she left in her drawer.

I mean, any one of these is a good-enough reason.
But he was right when he said that I was never good

at science. Maybe I shouldn't have worn
those flowered skirts and thought only of boys

and suffering. Was Marie the antidote?
Like my own mother to whom I wouldn't listen?

Once someone asked her
if she was a poet too, and she said, *No,*

with an expression of almost horror,
I'm a social scientist.

I gave my nephew a *Mama Llama* book for Christmas,
and my mother called to tell me she approves

of Mama Llama. Mama Llama doesn't like
melodrama. Well, of course she doesn't.

The rhyme was inevitable.
In the library at St. Aloysius Grade School,

there was a section of biographies of famous women
that included St. Theresa of the Little Flower,

Florence Nightingale, Clara Barton, and Marie Curie.
I checked them out again as soon as they were due.

Marie Curie was the one most famous for her mind.
Kindness was what my mother said

I had already, and this was clearly disappointing.
I think it would help if I had a band.

Like the Isotopes. I have never heard them but imagine
they are as clever as Bach's two-part inventions

which I always loved playing because you had to tell
one hand to do something completely different

than the other, not just complementary but distinct
and simultaneous. It is easy to think danger

is beautiful when you're not in it
or to love the thing you are discovering

when you don't yet know it's killing you.
I am discovering something. I can feel it coming closer.

Like the new year that is about to begin
in this late afternoon darkness,

the Christmas lights beaming sadly
after their time has passed, which is difficult

to determine while it's happening
but you know when it has.

I am skating on a pond I could fall through.
I wonder if Marie Curie was surprised

when she learned that science had deceived her.
I know she did not admit that radiation exposure

could have had anything to do
with her illness and death, which is in keeping

with her character, and thus another thing
I must admire.

What Has Lasted

Paris is the city where I've been
the loneliest, where once I didn't speak
to anyone for a week
so when I finally heard my voice again,
I sounded like someone else.
I stood beneath the Rose Windows
and through the shadows swirling with the dust
of centuries and the shadows panic made
in my mind, their beauty fell over me
like a silence, the good silence
a lake makes when the blue
fills up your eyes.

When I heard about the fire,
it was like one of those movies
when someone finally realizes
they love someone, but the someone
is getting on a plane at that very moment
so they have to rush to the airport
to try to stop them.
I guess I always thought it would be there,
the way it is my job now that my kids are grown
to keep going to work and making dinner
so when they call they will feel good,
knowing I am tending the dream of home.
But now that it is burning, I want to run
down Raspail up to Montparnasse,
past the Sorbonne and the Latin Quarter,
past Shakespeare and Co.
where it was always raining
and through the rain James Joyce
was whispering what it was like
to be an artist as a young man,

repeating the only line I remembered,
which was about kissing,
"Why do people do that with their two faces?"

I went to Paris on the money the government
gave my mother when my father died.
I didn't want to go, but she stood next to me
by the bookshelves in the basement
and said, *You're going*
because she had fought so hard
to make me someone who would want to.
When she came to visit me,
I took her to Notre Dame, and she wept and said,
I never thought I'd get here,
and we lit the votive candles for our dead
and walked along the stone walls
in a new kind of silence.
She was pleased with me then.
I wore the city like a scarf.

Today I watched the spire fall.
When I lived in Paris,
I was in love with someone
whom I thought of constantly.
Everything I saw I wanted to show him.
And now he is utterly gone.
What has lasted is the girl
running backwards across the stones,
all the way to 1991,
to wander that church again,
this time knowing there is no one to write to
who will make it easier to be alone.

Monica

We were having breakfast
for dinner, which is never good for me
because I don't like eggs,
and this seems to offend some people
but is not something I can fix.

Someone brought up Monica Lewinsky,
how she has a TED Talk now,
and then someone else asked if
it was about giving good blowjobs.
I said, *No, it's about shame.*

This was stronger than what
I usually do, but not strong enough,
so here I am, mechanical pencil
scraping away on the receipt
from the vet as I wait for the car wash,
trying to make amends.

When I was a child,
I had a friend named Monica
who painted my fingernails red.
When her mom saw,
she removed the polish right away
because *red was for hussies.*

Monica asked the audience
to raise their hands if they had not
done something when they were 22
that they regretted.

When I was 22,
I made the biggest mistake of my life.

I will never forgive myself
though I couldn't help it.
And the thing is
I don't have to tell you.

I should have said more
on Monica's behalf.
I sat at that table while people said
she should have changed her name,
and my husband was the one
who said that Monica pointed out
that Bill Clinton didn't have to.

I was mostly silent, staring at my nails,
which I had just gotten done that afternoon
to see if I could stop biting them.

When I was 22,
I had a rule that I could only bite
three a night because
more than three Band-Aids
looked like a problem.

But now my nails looked good.
The polish was clear
but had little flecks of glitter
that flashed like intelligence
when they caught the light.

Fleur de Lis

His name was Adonis
or that was his stage name—
you could tell he wasn't anyone specific.
The women climbed on him
and he barely noticed the way the right hand
has been instructed not to watch
what is given with the left.
The show was called *Hunks,*
and I had gotten there by a strange combination
of a bad day and a free ticket and a misconception.
I wore a dress patterned in fleur de lis
which my friend told me is the symbol of travel
when that was the charm I got in my piece
of bridesmaid cake at her wedding.
The sun was setting over the hills
when they pulled away in their Just Married car,
dragging its loud strings of cans.
All night I had been drinking beer and eating
tiny meatballs, wearing my peach dress
and dyed-to-match shoes
and dancing with my boyfriend who was realizing
he didn't want to marry me.
I didn't want to marry him either
though I would have
because I never know what I want or don't want
until it's too late.
Like at *Hunks* when the men walked out
into the audience and began giving lap dances,
even to women who hadn't paid.
My friend sobered up fast
when a man walked between us with nothing on.
She yelled at him not to touch us
and I said nothing.

Adonis stared at me from the stage
and said into the microphone
that if I didn't close my mouth
I would have a dick in it.
I was a challenge.
Adonis yanked back my chair.
My friend stood up and stuck her finger in his face.
I did nothing except sit there in my fleur de lis,
thinking I'll leave here someday.

The Neverending Story

I said I wasn't going to drive up one last time
to say goodbye to the house,
but the morning my parents' movers were coming,
I got out of bed and put on my exercise pants
with the stripes of flowers on the sides
and my shirt that says *Starstruck*
from an astronomy/poetry class I taught
and drove the two and half miles up the hill.

I hadn't wanted to cry.
Crying in middle age exacts a higher price.
In college, I was a champion crier,
second only to my friend Jen
who cried at least once a day
about something her boyfriend said
or how no one had done the dishes
or how she'd been up all night in the art studio
and nothing had turned out right.
Jen was a beautiful crier.
She would hold her fingers beneath her eyes
so her mascara wouldn't run,
and this was a kind of limit.

When I got to the house, my mother came
to the door and we could feel the last time
everywhere as I entered the echoing foyer,
gasped at the emptiness, the four chairs,
the bed stripped down.

My mother makes a bed beautifully,
flinging the sheet out so it hangs in the air
for a moment.
I used to love to watch her,
sitting in a pile of laundry on the floor.
Once I jumped on my own naked bed,

singing Billy Joel's "My Life."
Go ahead with your own life, leave me alone,
I sang, and we laughed,
imagining what it would be like
not to mean this as a joke.

My parents hand me boxes of random things
they're not taking with them, breadcrumbs,
packets of French onion soup mix, yard gnomes,
lavender hand soap, a Christmas cactus
my mother says actually blooms at Thanksgiving.
It prefers it, she adds.

My dad asks if I've hidden anything in the house.
Well, of course.
I didn't grow up here,
but I moved home during the worst year
of my life. I slept in the room up the stairs
to the left, with my youngest brother.
He had glow-in-the-dark stars on his ceiling
and a poster on the wall from *The Neverending Story.*
Once I lay face down on that bed in the daytime.
It was a Friday at five and the school
I had hoped would hire me had not called
so I knew I would have to wait the weekend now
to find out if I would have that job
or if I would have to take the one on the coast
in the small town in the woods
where the teacher had her own house
with a potbellied stove and grew old alone
in a story she could not get out of.
I was crying and my mother sat down beside me
and told me all the reasons I shouldn't,
how on Monday everything would work out.
I said, *But I'm sad,* and I thought then
she would leave, but instead she stopped talking
and put her hand on my back.

This Will Be the Last Day of My Life

The other day, one of my students mentioned
that he worked at Pete's Pizza for years.
At first, all I thought about was that twisty crust
all along the edge of their calzones, how good it is,
how it looks like the way the old woman Antonia
twists her hair in the film *Antonia's Line*,
you know the one where, in the first scene,
she wakes up and gets out of bed and announces,
in Dutch of course so the English words
are printed across the screen and my mind,
This will be the last day of my life.
My mother loves that movie because she loves movies
where people eat outside.
And in this one, I admit, it is especially
glorious, they're all at a long table with bread and wine
and the countryside.

After class, I remembered that I knew someone
who had also worked at Pete's, my best friend's
brother, that I had lost this friend, as sometimes happens,
I know now that I'm older.
She was in trouble and told me, *I can't be your friend
anymore because you ask me the questions
I ask myself in my mind.*

The next day, I asked my student about
my best friend's brother, and he said yes,
he knew him, and then he looked at me
because he knew what I was really asking,
which was did he know that he had died?

I think I always knew that my friend and I
were only sitting outside at that long and elegant table
for a while.
We slept on the trampoline in her parents' back yard,
rolling into each other in the middle,
studying the stars without speaking of them
because we knew the stars were the night's silence,
like in a story when the narrator tells you
what things look like for a while,
and the characters can just be quiet.

My friend was getting married
and she hadn't known me long
but she asked me to be one of her bridesmaids.
She said she had bridesmaids who represented
all the parts of who she was, and that I could be
the smart one. I think of this sometimes
when I'm teaching *The Awakening*
and I talk about the female characters who serve
as Edna's foils. I draw a flower on the board and write
Edna inside it and then I draw vines out from it
for Madame Ratignolle and Mademoiselle Reisz
and Madame Lebrun and the Lady in Black,
and I say, *These are the bridesmaids*.

This will be the last day of my life, I think sometimes
in the mornings when I regard myself in the mirror
like Antonia.

I am sorry for my friend's loss and also
that I asked her those questions
she didn't want spoken out loud.
I needed to learn how to look at the stars
and not say anything
because we were out in the country
where there were no lights.

Dear Baby,

You are a small horse,
and I am a human,
so I'm not sure you will ever read this.
But just in case, I want you to know
that I laughed when Maya pointed out
you were standing in a corner
right after we learned your name
and then realized you did not
understand the reference
and then thought there is so much
you don't understand
and then thought that actually
it's both of us.
Though I've come to this farm
in these overalls I just got
for my 51st birthday, I do not know
much about animals.
Ellen just reminded me I am one,
and I felt the little hairs on my arms.
Ellen told us your heart is on
the wrong side of your body
and that you have scoliosis.
But you don't know this
so you run faster than
all the other tiny horses.
I almost gasped when Ellen said
the part about how you don't know,
but because I'm human,
I caught the gasp
before it came out.
Lately, I've been thinking a lot
about *Dirty Dancing*, the scene
where Baby says she's afraid

of walking out of that room
and never feeling like that again.
And also the part after that when
she's trying to put on her stockings
before the final night at Kellerman's
and suddenly the task is too hard,
drawing the thin nylons all the way up
her legs without tearing them,
and her sister who is like all sisters
just a creature she has accidentally been
given to love sits down next to her
and Baby puts her head on her shoulder.
I feel these two things often:
like I've missed out on my greatest love
and like it might have been here
all the time. Ellen's daughter Delia
tells us that S'more is Baby's best friend.
S'more is of course black and brown
and white. Well, not of course.
Delia says that the blonde horse
is named Ginger and the ginger horse
is named Winter and shrugs.
I do prefer it when things
don't make sense.
I am here with my son.
He is the tallest among us, Baby,
so I'm sure you've noticed him.
He has a mane of dark curly hair
and eyes you want to come up close to.
He is grown so he is not always
with me now.
On the drive up, I tell him
that I still feel him beside me
when he's gone inside his own life.
Ellen says the whole point
of rescuing these animals is so

they can die.
Not be slaughtered. Die.
In a pile of hay
where Nigel the pig sleeps
because he has nightmares.
Baby, you should tell the other Baby
what you know
though you and I both know
she won't listen:
a restless heart is not a plight.

Shogun

I called my mother to say goodbye
because she was leaving for Europe in the morning.

She said, *This is my last trip,* and she meant to Europe,
but I misunderstood for a moment.

What does the world feel like without your mother?
So many things that only she wants to know.

Like the fact that Shogun burned down.
The old Japanese restaurant
where my brother took his date for prom.
My brother lives in Japan now. We never see him.

The fire made Shogun look like a hole in your gum
where you lost a permanent tooth,
which was not permanent, turns out.

I should mention Shogun to my mother when she gets back.
They used to cook the food right at the tables, she will say,
shaking her head, as if that makes it worse that it's gone.

ACKNOWLEDGMENTS

I'm grateful to the following journals, where versions of many of these poems were published:

Beloit Poetry Journal: "RIP, Laura's Vagina"
Blood Orange Review: "Erin," "In the same way we misunderstand the child ballerinas of Degas," "The Whole History of Femininity"
Cimarron Review: "The Milkmaid," "Solving for X"
Dogwood: "Margaret Corinne, Dunseith, North Dakota, 1932"
Fugue: "Yesterday"
Gettysburg Review: "Dear Baby," "Fleur de Lis," "What Has Lasted"
Kenyon Review: "Jane Doe 1–9
Laurel Review: "Marie Curie and the Isotopes, World Tour, 1911," "This Will Be the Last Day of My Life"
Lilac City Fairy Tales: "The Pea"
Moss: "The Lucky Penny"
On the Seawall: "Clever Dress," "Maya Miller," "Music Box"
Poetry Northwest: "Deer are the obvious stand-ins for the dead," "The Fourth Wall," "Is it to preserve the heat of the body?"
Radar: "Jellyfish," *"We're out of tin, we have aluminum"*
Rattle: "The Cheerleader," "Phallogocentric"
Redivider: "Quince"
Stirring: "Elegy with Sammy Hagar and *Beauty and the Beast*"
Westchester Review: "American Realism"
Willow Springs: "Neither Bride nor Daughter"

The epigraph for "In the same way we misunderstand the child ballerinas of Degas" comes from Germaine Greer, "Artists have always glamorized prostitution. Manet savaged all their delusions," *Guardian,* February 6, 2011.

Many thanks to Ellen Doré Watson for choosing this book as the winner of the Juniper Prize; to the University of Massachusetts

Press for publishing it; to Kate Lebo, Kathryn Nuernberger, Kat Smith, Alexandra Teague, Ellen Welcker, and Maya Jewell Zeller for reading and helping me with these poems along the way; and to my family for providing me with the material and the love necessary for the making of poems.